BUDDHA
FOR BEGINNERS™

STEPHEN T. ASMA IS A PROFESSOR OF PHILOSOPHY AT COLUMBIA COLLEGE CHICAGO

WRITERS AND READERS PUBLISHING, INC.

P.O. Box 461, Village Station
New York, NY 10014

Writers and Readers Limited
9 Cynthia Street
London N1 9JF
England

•

Text and Illustrations Copyright: © Stephen T. Asma
Cover & Book Design: Peter Altenberg
Assistant Book Design: Stacey Ruderman

A Writers and Readers Documentary Comic Book
Copyright © 1996
ISBN # 0-86316-186-3 Trade
2 3 4 5 6 7 8 9 0

Manufactured in the United States of America

Beginners Documentary Comic Books are published by Writers and Readers Publishing, Inc. Its trademark, consisting of the words "For Beginners, Writers and Readers Documentary Comic Books" and the Writers and Readers logo, is registered in the U. S. Patent and Trademark Office and in other countries.

Writers and Readers—
publishing FOR BEGINNERS™ books
continuously since 1975:

1975: Cuba • 1976: Marx • 1977: Lenin • 1978: Nuclear Power • 1979: Einstein • Freud • 1980: Mao • Trotsky • 1981: Capitalism • 1982: Darwin • Economists • French Revolution • Marx's Kapital • French Revolution • Food • Ecology • 1983: DNA • Ireland • 1984: London • Peace • Medicine • Orwell • Reagan • Nicaragua • Black History • 1985: Marx Diary • 1986: Zen • Psychiatry • Reich • Socialism • Computers • Brecht • Elvis • 1988: Architecture • Sex • JFK • Virginia Woolf • 1990: Nietzsche • Plato • Malcolm X • Judaism • 1991: WW II • Erotica • African History • 1992: Philosophy • Rainforests • Malcolm X • Miles Davis • Islam • Pan Africanism • 1993: Psychiatry • Black Women • Arabs & Israel • Freud • 1994: Babies • Foucault • Heidegger • Hemingway • Classical Music • 1995: Jazz • Jewish Holocaust • Health Care • Domestic Violence • Sartre • United Nations • Black Holocaust • Black Panthers • Martial Arts • History of Clowns • 1996: Opera • Biology • Saussure • UNICEF • Kierkegaard • Addiction & Recovery • I Ching • Buddha • Derrida • Chomsky • McLuhan • Jung • 1997: Lacan • Shakespeare • Structuralism

---

Acknowledgments

I wish to express my thanks to Peter Altenberg for his excellent work as designer of the book. Thanks also to Stacey Ruderman for assistant design. This book would not have been possible without the advice and support of my wife Heidi, whose sense of humor inspires many of its pages. A special thanks to those friends, family and teachers who understood that laughter is the proper response to the sacrosanct. This book is dedicated to my parents Ed and Carol, who must be Bodhisattvas in disguise.

"BEGINNER'S MIND"

Contents

BUDDHA
FOR BEGINNERS™

WRITTEN AND ILLUSTRATED BY
STEPHEN T. ASMA

Writers and Readers

Chapter 1: The Quest of the Young Prince

J UST AS THERE ARE MANY forms of Christianity in the West, so too there are many different manifestations of Buddhism in the East. But just as there was supposedly one Jesus who lived and taught in Galilee almost two thousand years ago, so again was there one historically real man who walked the Northern Indian landscape and became the "Buddha" (Enlightened One). His name was Siddhartha Gautama and this book is primarily concerned with introducing him and his teachings rather than the whole spectrum of later Buddhist developments.

The West becomes enchanted with Buddhism in what seem like cycles of searching spiritualism. In the nineteenth century, American and Continental Transcendentalists recognized the wisdom of Buddhism and sought to deal with it in some fashion. In the "Beat" era of this century, every bongo-playing poet had a copy of Buddhist scriptures in his pocket.

And lamentably, in this day of the "New Age" every occult thing from "crystal healing" to psychic spoon-bending is spuriously linked with Buddhism or "Eastern Spirituality." Thankfully, the historical Buddha was not as silly as the recent superstitions that illegitimately intone his name.

Gautama was born in the Ganges Valley near Gorakhpur between Nepal in the North and Varanasi (Benares) in the South.

He was born in 563 BCE to king Suddhodana and his wife Maya (both from the tribe of Shakyas), and legend has it that when he was born a "seer" foretold that he would one day leave his family to wander as an ascetic holy man. Suddhodana feared that the prophesy might come to pass and, after Maya's early death, he and Gautama's aunt Prajapati sought to shelter the boy from the world outside the palace. Lest Gautama be lured away, the over-protective parents surrounded the young prince with every kind of luxury and sought to insulate him from any images of suffering.

Being a prince and enjoying the benefits of such a station, Gautama undoubtedly received a fine education and of course a share of Brahmanic spiritual tutoring in the Upanishads and Vedic Hindu scriptures. But perhaps not too much spiritual tutoring since Suddhodana hoped for the kind of pragmatic and common-sensical heir that might one day succeed his rule.

Eventually, Gautama
married his cousin
Yosodhara
and they
had a son named
Rahula.

The family lived
peacefully and
pleasurably, but in a
state of happy
ignorance about the
world at large.

In time, however, the prince glimpsed the suffering and death of human beings outside, beyond the palace walls, and this new awareness awakened a compassion for his fellow human beings and a distaste for his current sheltered privilege. Gautama's increasing concern with the suffering of human beings is crystallized in a legendary episode wherein he experiences for the first time an elderly and decrepit man,

then a maimed individual...

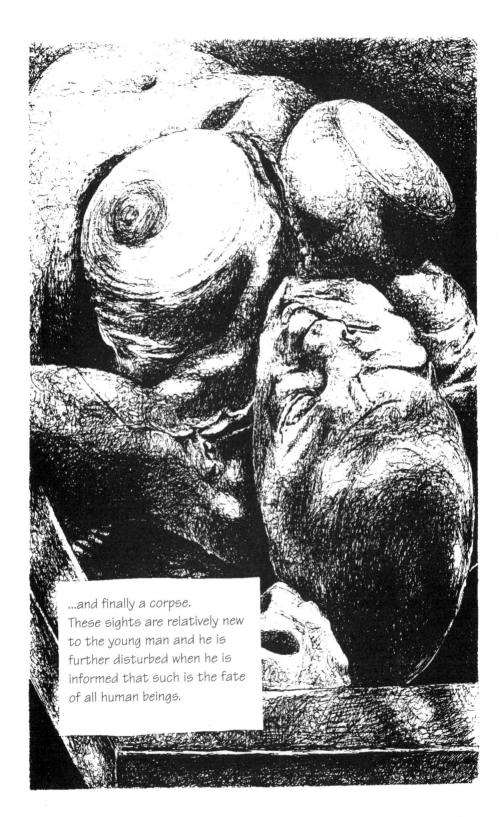

...and finally a corpse.
These sights are relatively new
to the young man and he is
further disturbed when he is
informed that such is the fate
of all human beings.

Though sources regarding Gautama's family life are scant, we have every reason to believe that he was a loving husband and father. Somewhere in the back of his mind, however, was a restless sense of incompleteness and an increasingly overpowering empathy for less fortunate people. How could he remain in his artificial bliss, he thought, when the world around him was suffering? And how could he continue to ignore the brute fact that his beloved wife and son would one day wither into suffering infirmity and death?

With the goal of discovering the truth about life and death, Gautama resolved to leave behind his home and family and to return only after he had procured the antidote. Late one night, when he was 29 years old, Gautama gazed long upon his sleeping wife and child and then quietly departed from the palace. Thus did he relinquish everything he had known and loved up to that point in his life.

It is an interesting paradox that in order for Gautama to become enlightened and cure the puzzle of human suffering, he had to cause more of it by leaving his family.

In order to understand the course of Gautama's spiritual journey, it is important to appreciate the philosophical and religious context of India at the time. The Hindu system of beliefs is very diverse but their common roots are in the ancient scriptures known as the Upanishads (circa 900-200 BCE) and the older Vedas (dating as far back as 1200 BCE).

The Vedic scriptures are the outgrowth of an ideological and cultural clash that occurred during the second millennium BCE. Aryans from the North invaded and conquered the indigenous peoples of India starting around 1700 BCE. This clash produced a rich fusion of traditions and the resulting theology, dominated by Aryan divinities, was articulated in the hymns collectively known as the Vedas (perhaps, the most notable being the cosmogony work, the Rig Veda). What is known of the original non-Aryan culture is sketchy but important. For example, the original religious orientation was fairly ascetic and egalitarian. That is to say, more stress was laid upon each individual's spiritual struggle against the distractions of bodily existence, than upon an articulated theology and attendant priest hierarchy. These non-Aryan dimensions gain greater weight in the later Hinduism of the Upanishad period.

The Vedic literature
develops the basic
pantheon of Hinduism.
A trinity of gods,
Brahma, Vishnu and
Shiva, forms the hub
of Hindu beliefs.

Brahma is a kind of non personal first-principle for all creation, while Vishnu (the preserver) and Shiva (the destroyer) are subjects of many mythologies. Vishnu is the cosmic principle that holds reality in existence, while Shiva transforms reality into novel forms by bringing about destruction. The three deities are religious manifestations of the endless natural cycles of generation and corruption, birth and death. Later Hindu texts (after the death of Buddha) like the *Bhagavad Gita* and *Ramayana* continue the theology of Vishnu in different incarnations like "Krishna" and "Rama" respectively.

In the time of Gautama, the Vedic traditions had grown increasingly ritualistic, and a class of priests, known as Brahmins, had developed into the established peddlers of religious truth.

The Vedic tradition embraced an "anatomical" metaphor for a sanctified social order or caste system. The Brahmin or priest class represented the "head" of an organism; the warrior and the class of nobility represented the "arms"; the merchant and craft class represented the "thighs"; and the peasant class represented the "feet." It was imperative, according to Hindu thought, that individuals of each caste resign themselves to their respective stations in the cosmic order.

We know that Gautama became rather hostile towards the priest-class and eventually preached against the common practices of ritual animal sacrifice and hollow ceremony. Gautama's social status can not be entirely irrelevant to this issue as well. For there was a strong emphasis in the Upanishad literature, written in the centuries before and during Gautama's life, upon the warrior and the princely class (ksatriyas) of which Gautama belonged. This emphasis indicates the general devaluation of the Brahmin class from their previous privilege, and it may give insight into the Buddha's eventual healthy distrust of authority.

The impact of the Upanishads upon Hinduism was to revitalize the pre-Aryan dimensions of the culture. The Aryan culture was more worldly than ascetic – their religious ceremonies, for example, exalted the use of intoxicants (soma) and stressed the power of sacrifice and prayer to manipulate the gods. The idea that the gods could be bribed for gifts and intoned as curses upon enemies became questioned by the tradition-challenging rationalism of some of the Upanishad writings, and the Buddha's eventual claim that human beings "save" themselves ultimately completed this rejection of prayerful groveling and sacrificial bargaining.

Brahmin rituals increasingly became vehicles by which people could seek earthly benefits.

In addition to the distrust of priestly authority, the Upanishads reintroduced (probably from pre-Aryan times) an important non-Vedic doctrine into Hinduism, reincarnation or transmigration. Transmigration (samsara) is the idea that after death, one is reborn into a new physical body and life continues on. The laws that dictate what kind of rebirth one might expect are summarized as "karma" (consequences of actions).

Samsara and Karma are basic principles of Hinduism, and as such the historical Buddha was more than familiar with them.

When Gautama left his home and family he first sought spiritual guidance from a famous Brahman named Arada Kalama. Arada taught that the self or "atman" was an eternal soul that one could eventually release, over many life-times, from the bondage of material existence. Apparently, the Buddha was unimpressed with the teachings of Arada and sought further instruction under the guru Udraka Ramaputra.

Udraka also taught that belief in an underlying spiritual "self" or soul was crucial to a healthy moral pathway. It was this underlying immaterial self that transmigrated after death and if karma determined one's future life, then one would act morally upright now in order to protect one's self down the road. But again Gautama was unimpressed with this doctrine of a transmigrating substantial soul, and left the Brahmans to search elsewhere.

TRAVELING SOUTH TOWARDS GAYA, GAUTAMA CAME IN CONTACT WITH HOLY MEN WHO PRACTICED A FORM OF ASCETICISM KNOWN AS JAINISM.

JAINISM EH? WHAT'S IT ALL ABOUT BOB?

The Jains were an offshoot of mainstream Hinduism, distinctly heterodox in the sense that they basically ignored the Vedas and the Brahmins who interpreted them. They embraced the doctrine of karma and the dualistic metaphysics of matter and spirit, but they moved away from ritu-al and scholarly religion in favor of moral action. Actually, for the Jain, the highest moral action is no action at all. This is because all life is a rela-tion between souls and matter, and it is matter that is ruled by chains of karmic causality. To act at all, say you cook up a steak for dinner, is to set in motion some chain of events that will come back at you and thereby keep you in the game of material life. According to the Jain, the killing and eating of this animal has cre-ated a causal chain of pain that will inex-orably lead back to its originator. In this way, one's spiritual self cannot get free of one's material (karma-determined) self. The solution to this predicament, accord-ing to Jainism, is to act as little as pos-sible — only in this way will one be released from the cycles of causality and pain. The lifestyle of the Jain is monastic and incredibly austere. Only through austere non-action can one annihilate karmic matter and thereby allow the soul to rise to its nat-ural state of tranquil bliss.

Gautama adopted this ascetic lifestyle and through self-denial and non-action he sought to learn the truth about the human condition. Like other extreme ascetics, he probably filtered his drinking water to avoid accidentally ingesting and killing small life forms; he may have worn breathing masks to stop the inadvertent breathing of insects; he walked carefully to avoid stepping on a life; and he starved himself as a negation of the bodily drives that lead to karmic imprisonment. The ultimate goal of this life is to have the self-control and discipline   to simply fast oneself to death.

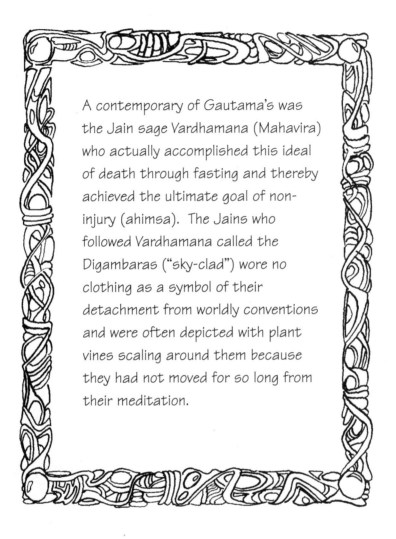

A contemporary of Gautama's was the Jain sage Vardhamana (Mahavira) who actually accomplished this ideal of death through fasting and thereby achieved the ultimate goal of non-injury (ahimsa). The Jains who followed Vardhamana called the Digambaras ("sky-clad") wore no clothing as a symbol of their detachment from worldly conventions and were often depicted with plant vines scaling around them because they had not moved for so long from their meditation.

ALRIGHT, LET'S GET A LEAF ON IT SON

For six years Gautama practiced ascetic self-denial and withered to a walking corpse. One day, while bathing in the river, his strength failed him and he collapsed into the water. If not for an overhanging branch, Gautama would have drowned from his inability to overcome the gentle current.

After regaining the shore, he collapsed and lay suffering until a young woman named Sujata discovered him and returned with nourishment.

On that day Gautama realized that his life of austerity had revealed no deep truths to his searching mind, in fact the starvation and dehydration had only distracted and diverted him from spiritual understanding. He vowed to lay down the life of extreme asceticism and henceforth to nourish the body as a part of the true path. The life of self-negation was as extreme and unproductive as his previous life of incessant luxury.

THE MIDDLE WAY

Finally, Gautama came to a tree and resolved to sit beneath it and meditate his way to perfect truth. Using an intense yogic concentration that he must have first acquired in his ascetic phase and from his early gurus, Gautama fell into a deep trance-state. After many hours he was able to detach from his senses, his emotions and his desires. Next he entered a state of pure inner consciousness and awareness, and ultimately a non-conscious ecstasy. In that ecstasy, he grasped the elusive cause of suffering, the pathway around suffering and the nature of supreme peace (nirvana). That day Gautama became the Buddha (the enlightened one).

The Buddha went on to share his insights, gathering large numbers of disciples throughout the area of Varanasi. He taught them the Dharma, the path or system of correct living that would free them from suffering (dukkha). He argued that enlightenment was available to everyone. Neither a priest-class nor a transcendent God bestowed truth upon the searcher. Attaining nirvana is ultimately within the power of all human beings – human beings save themselves through the highly disciplined path that Gautama first discovered. Subsequently, it is not the Buddha himself that is of paramount importance, rather, it is the path itself.

What, exactly, is the Buddha's philosophy?

Chapter II: The Wheel of Becoming

THE RELATIONSHIP BETWEEN THE BUDDHA'S PHILOSOPHY AND Hinduism is complex. When the traditional mythology of the Vedas was examined and developed in the Upanishads, Indian philosophy became focused upon the nature of Brahman (God as "first cause"). And more importantly, Hindu thinkers attempted to articulate the relationship between Brahman and each individual person's soul or self — in Sanskrit, "Atman." Are we, as individual persons, related to the Godhead in some way?

The symbol for "Om," the Hindu mantra representing the imperishable sound of the universe.

Unlike the Judeo-Christian God, Brahman has no anthropomorphic personality.

God, in the Upanishads, is the creative originating principle for the entire cosmos. All of nature is in a relentless state of flux or becoming. Animals grow old and perish, seasons come and go, political empires pass away, solar systems arise and collapse. . .

. . . and bell-bottoms go in and out of fashion. All these things make up the ever-changing world of "Becoming", but these are really only manifestations of the all-encompassing reality. The all-encompassing foundation is Being itself or Brahman, which is the source of all created things. Underlying all the changes of the natural world lies the changeless essential reality of God.

The relationship between Brahman and Nature is different from the Western conception. Most Western theologians (with some few exceptions, like Spinoza) picture God as "outside" the cosmos — transcending above and beyond His created object (the universe). Like a skilled watchmaker who stands apart from her created time piece, God stands apart from the created cosmos. In the West, God might occasionally step into the mundane realm to wind His clock — perhaps making a statue or two weep miraculously — but generally speaking the Deity is unsullied by the material world.

In the Hindu tradition, however, God is not only the antecedent and transcendent world-maker, Brahman is also the world itself. The natural world around us, that we encounter on a daily basis, is not simply God's created artifact — it is Brahman itself. The natural world is just a manifestation of God and the two cannot really be separated.

In the Chandogya Upanishad (VI. 13. 1), the novice Svetaketu asks his sage father Aruni how God can be present everywhere and yet go undetected by the senses. Aruni demonstrates with an analogy.

"Place this salt in the water and come to me in the morning"

"That salt you placed in the water last evening, please bring it here."

He looked for the salt but could not find it because it had completely dissolved.

"Please take a sip of it from this end. How is it?"

"Salt."

"Take a sip from the middle. How is it?"

"Salt."

"Take a sip from the other end. How is it?"

"Salt!"

It is always the same.

Like the salt that infuses all of the water but remains unseen, so too Brahman is the omnipresent yet invisible principle of reality.

"Verily, indeed, my dear, you do not perceive Pure Being here. Verily, indeed, it is here."

More important for understanding the Buddha's philosophical revolution is the related Hindu concept of Atman or "soul." Just as there is this permanent essential reality underlying Nature called Being or Brahman, there is also an unchanging permanent dimension of human beings — namely, Atman. The principal lesson of the Upanishads is that both the fluctuating cosmos and the ever-changing material human body are only distracting veils (maya) over the important spiritual reality. In the case of human beings, there is a changeless soul or "ego" that provides the continuity beneath the fleeting material person.

Atman, though unseen and unheard, is the "ruling" part of the individual creature. It is this subtle essence – this immutable core self – that makes up the true self. And in a famous phrase from the Upanishads, the sage Aruni repeatedly explains the Atman to Svetaketu and proclaims "That art thou" (tat tvam asi).

A person is not their color, or their blood, or their flesh, or even their brain. These are all ephemeral compared with Atman.

In other words, one shouldn't get hung up on the trivial trials and tribulations of one's daily life, for all of it will pass. But the core self will always remain through this life and the next and the next.

It is the self or ego that migrates from one body and lifetime to another. Karma is both produced (kartr) and received (bhoktr) throughout different lifespans by this eternal self – it is the "agent" and "patient" of karma. Much like the Western concept of an afterlife, there is something psychologically soothing about the idea that one's essential self will live beyond this lifetime.

The last, and perhaps most difficult, part of Hindu philosophy for us to understand is the relationship between Brahman and Atman. Brahman is God and Atman is the individual self, but in a deeper sense they are both the same thing.

SAY WHAT?

Most properly speaking, there is only one permanent reality and that is God, but the individual selves are manifestations or expressions of God temporarily separated from itself. There is an ideal unity of the soul of the human (Atman) and the soul of the universe (Brahman). Individual selves are related to God like sparks to a fire. . .

. . . or water droplets to the sea - they are not qualitatively different and yet they are temporarily estranged from each other.

So why does God break itself up into individual egos? What's the point of it all?

The transcendent unmanifested Brahman does not need to achieve liberation from ignorance, because it is already completely perfected and free. But the eternally Divine God seeks to express itself through many conscious selves because in this way it is able to rise above ignorance. As the cosmic play unfolds, human egos continue to conquer the challenges of living and realize self-knowledge. With this conquering of ignorance we are reunited with the Universal Consciousness and this saga is one of the infinite expressions that flow from Brahman.

The aim of the Cosmic Dance is to celebrate itself.

Having explored the basic metaphysics of Hindu philosophy, we can better understand both the similarities and the radical differences with Buddha's teachings. The most shocking break from previous thinking is the Buddha's rejection of the concept of "self."

One of the central, and least understood, concepts of the Buddha's philosophy is the doctrine of "no-self" (anatman). The Hindu philosophy correctly pointed out the impermanent nature of the human body and the fallibility of the senses and the fleeting character of daily consciousness. But despite all this flux and alteration, an inner agent, Atman, persisted. The Buddha embraced this theory of the impermanence of all things but pushed the theory further than the Upanishads and claimed that this supposedly permanent self, Atman, was itself a fiction. Just as the Upanishad philosophers reprimanded people for thinking that the changing material world was reality, the Buddha now reprimanded the Upanishad philosophers for thinking that the self was reality.

To argue that there is no immortal self is to pull a very comforting rug out from under religious thinking. The idea that some part of us lives on and on is pleasing and satisfies our craving for immortality. According to the Buddha, however, satisfying cravings is not the path to truth.

Not only is there no evidence for an immortal self, but to believe in its existence, according to the Buddha, will lead to an immoral life. It leads to evil because such a belief is ultimately ego-centered and selfish, and human beings will be unable to free themselves if they are seeking rewards in their future lives.

In the Samyutta Nikaya, the Buddha states:

"All formations are transient; all formations are subject to suffering; all things are without a self (anatman). Form is transient, feeling is transient, perception is transient, mental formations are transient, consciousness is transient."

According to the Buddha, realizing and understanding that we have no immortal self or soul is part of the enlightenment process – it is a feature of our awakening.

"Suppose, a man, who can see, were to behold the many bubbles on the Ganges as they are driving along. And he should watch them and carefully examine them. After carefully examining them, they will appear to him as empty, unreal, and unsubstantial.

In exactly the same way does the monk behold all the bodily forms, feelings, perceptions, mental formations and states of consciousness – whether they be of the past, or the present, or the future, far or near. And he watches them and examines them carefully, and, after carefully examining them, they appear to him as empty, void and without a self." (S.21, 6)

The Buddha rejects the idea of a substantial self that migrates from body to body — there is nothing like an immaterial soul (whether it be Christian, Hindu or Platonic) that can exist independently of body. In the Majjhima Nikaya, Buddha states: "It is impossible that any one can explain the passing out of one existence and the entering into a new existence. . . independent of bodily form, feeling, perception and mental formation." (28) The immaterial self is an unverifiable fiction.

In the Brhadaranyaka Upanishad (2.4.5) the self is said to underlie the veneer of daily life. "Not for the sake of the husband is the husband loved, but for the sake of the self is the husband loved. Not for the sake of the wife is the wife loved, but for the sake of the self is the wife loved. Not for the sake of the sons are the sons loved, but for the sake of the self are the sons loved." But the Buddha points out that invoking the self in this way really adds nothing to our understanding – nothing is added by positing a self behind every thought or feeling.

In the Majjhima Nikaya, Buddha states:

"If there really existed the Ego, there would be also something that belonged to the Ego. As, however, in truth and reality, neither an Ego nor anything belonging to an Ego can be found, is it therefore not really an utter fool's doctrine to say: This is the world, this am I; after death I shall be permanent, persisting and eternal?"(22)

But far more shocking than the idea that no substantial self exists *between* lives is the Buddha's claim that neither does a substantial self exist *within* a lifetime.

WHAT !?
IS THERE **NO** ROLE LEFT FOR ME TO PLAY ?

The ego that ties together all of one's perceptions and feelings and thoughts is figmentary, according to the Buddha. Contrary to Descartes, we cannot deduce the existence of an "I" from the act of thinking (cogitating). A person is really only a bundle of perceptions.

RENE

There is nothing "substantially" the same in my childhood and adulthood, but the causal process itself gives a kind of continuity between bundles of thoughts and impressions.

The Buddha dispels the myth of the metaphysical self (atman) as an underlying entity through life spans and between life spans. But he understands that each person feels a sense of themself as a self or ego. This palpable experience of the "I" is not completely illusory, for the Buddha claims that it is produced out of the combinations or conjunctions of feeling (vedana), perception (sanna), disposition (sankhara), consciousness (vinnana) and body (rupa). These are the five aggregates (khanda) or bundles of personhood and though each of these is impermanent and always fluctuating, they combine into the "felt" sense of the personal ego.

Interestingly enough, the Buddha did not turn to a purely Materialistic philosophy after he decried the existence of Atman. There was a school of Indian philosophy prior to the Buddha, founded by Carvaka (date unknown), which held that all knowledge came exclusively from the senses (like the Greek Sophist Protagoras) and all reality was comprised exclusively of the material elements. This school, later known as Lokayata ("belonging to the world of sense"), argued that the spirit or soul is nothing but a momentary organization of material

elements and when the body dies, so too the spirit. They opposed the concept of Karma and the transmigration of souls (samsara) on the grounds that these were based upon philosophical inferences rather than sense perceptions.

All the rituals and teachings of the Brahmans were considered to be the work of charlatans, and the Lokayata supposedly gave themselves over to the life of sensual gratification. The cause and effect of the material world impinging upon our perception was considered to be the final word concerning the nature of existence.

Though the Buddha did reject the reality of "self", there are two important reasons why this did not lead him to a purely materialistic philosophy. The first point, which will be taken up in detail in the next chapter, is that the Buddha's entire conception of freedom is to break away from causality itself. Gratification of the senses, as the Materialists recommended, is the sure path to attachment and slavery.

Secondly, the Buddha, in rejecting Atman, never rejected the truth of karma or transmigration. While it is true that a higher moral law (karma) is not something sensed in the normal way (sight, hearing, smelling, touching and tasting), its truth was not just an inference for the Buddha. Materialists dismissed karma on the grounds that it could not be experienced through the senses, but the Buddha's intensive yogic training allowed him to intuit or perceive truths in meditation without the traditional five senses. The Buddha developed a sixth sense, as it were, which allowed him to see the reality of karma and transmigration — he "perceived" rather than "conceived" the wheel of becoming. This might be akin to the Saints of the West actually "seeing" or "feeling" God (Revealed Theology) rather than "arguing" for It's existence (Natural Theology).

This is where Buddhism becomes extremely difficult to grasp, for if there is no substantial self, then, What exactly transmigrates? What exactly is the subject and object of karma? If there is no self, then how can I go on to a next life and be held responsible for actions in this life? Indeed, if I am not the person I was a year ago or even two days ago, then how can praise or blame concerning past actions be fixed to me — for I am no longer that person who helped an elderly woman across the street two days ago?

The Buddha tries, in the Digha Nikaya, to explain this difficulty with a simile. He shows that each new moment of time brings a different reality, but the birth of each new reality is dependent upon its predecessor. There is a sequence which forms a continuity between lives such that karma inexorably follows, yet properly speaking each successive reality is different from another.

"Just as from the cow comes the milk, from the milk comes the curds . . .

. . . from curds butter, from butter ghee, from ghee the scum (of ghee); and when it is milk, it is not counted as curds or butter or ghee or scum of ghee, but only as milk; and when it is curds it is only counted as curds.

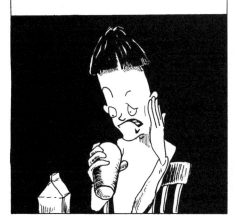

Even so was my past existence at that time real, but unreal the future and present existence; and my future existence will be at one time real, but unreal the past and present existence; and my present existence is now real, but unreal the past and future existence. All these are mere popular designations and expressions, mere conventional terms of speaking, mere popular notions."(9)

There is no self that unites these different "bundles of perception" (persons) through lifetimes, but each one is still causally connected to its previous reality. And this is how karma can work without appeal to the concept of Atman. The milk necessarily precedes the existence of ghee – there is a causal connection between the two different substances. So too, past, present and future lives are tied together by the sequential law of cause and effect.

A few hundred years after the Buddha's death, the Buddhist sage Nagasena attempted to clarify this puzzling doctrine for the argumentative Bactrian King Milinda. King Milinda seeks to understand how the doctrine of no-self can be reconciled with that of karma.

"When someone is reborn, Venerable Nagasena, is he the same as the one who just died, or is he another?"

"He is neither the same nor another."

"Give me a simile!"

"If a man were to light a lamp, could it give light throughout the whole night?"

Yes it could

Is now the flame which burns in the first watch of the night the same as the one which burns in the second?

It is not the same

Or is the flame which burns in the second watch the same as the one which burns in the last one?

It is not the same.

Do we then take it that there is one lamp in the first watch of the night, another in the second, and another again in the third?

No, it is because of just that one lamp that the light shines throughout the night.

And so like the lamp, we must understand the juxtaposition of a series of successive lives. At rebirth one life arises, while another stops; but the two processes take place almost simultaneously (i.e. they are continuous).

Another simile may also help us understand this difficult doctrine. Imagine a lifespan as a lit candle. Now take that candle and light another candle, immediately blowing out the first candle. Repeat this process several times, each time lighting a new candle and extinguishing the previous. It seems absurd to say that the flame at the end of the process is the same flame as the first lit candle. It is not one identical flame that gets passed along, in fact the flame is different from itself at each moment even while it burns on one candle. But there is a definite causal relationship uniting the first and last candles. Karma links earlier and later lives together in the same way that the different flames are linked together — but there is no "one substance" (self) which continues throughout.

Having made these radical metaphysical changes to traditional Indian philosophy, the Buddha refused to engage in further metaphysical speculation and focused his energies on freeing people through moral action from the chains of suffering. Much of the Buddha's moral teachings presupposes this intricate metaphysics, but he knew that the masses of people who were uninitiated in the subtleties of Hindu scholarship could simply ignore these subtleties and move on to the process of awakening themselves.

So, now that we have seen what the "wheel of becoming" actually is, let us find out how one escapes from it. For unlike most Western religions, the Buddha does not want immortality or everlasting life. To the contrary, Buddhism seeks to stop the afterlife. The goal of Buddhism is to be annihilated – to blow out one's flame.

Chapter III: Nirvana & the Noble Truths

WHILE ONE MUST EVENTUALLY DEVELOP DEEP philosophical powers of reflection, a doctorate in Hindu metaphysics is not a necessary prerequisite for enlightenment. The Buddha holds that one can embark upon the righteous path without first resolving every cosmic puzzle. Buddhism is a strenuously practical philosophy which, very similar to the attitude of Socrates in the West, stressed individual moral development over pure theory.

The Buddha characterizes this philosophical preference with an analogy in the Majjhima Nikaya text (63).

"Should anyone say that he does not wish to lead the righteous life under the Enlightened One, unless the Enlightened One first tells him, whether the world is eternal or temporal, finite or infinite; whether the life principle is identical with the body, or sometimes different; whether the Perfect One continues after death etc. – Such a person would die, before the Perfect One could tell him all this. It is as if a man were pierced by a poisoned arrow, and his friends, companions, or near relations called in a surgeon but that man should say: I will not have this arrow pulled out until I know who the man is that has wounded me: whether he is a noble, a prince, a citizen, or a servant; or whether he is tall, or short, or of medium height. Truly, such a man would die, before he could adequately learn all this."

74

In all of his thinking and teaching, the Buddha never loses sight of his pragmatic original mission which is to find the cure for human suffering. The most important key to understanding the path to enlightenment is that set of Buddha's teachings (dharma) known as the Four Noble Truths.

Meditating beneath that tree in the Ganges Valley, Gautama awakened to the First Noble Truth, which is: All life is permeated with suffering (dukkha). To live is to suffer.

This appears at first to be a deeply pessimistic outlook, but the Buddha is simply stating that a variety of pains and misfortunes accompany the human condition. For example, in possessing a body every human being is open to the suffering of degeneration (getting sick, growing old, etc.), and having a family and friends means that we are all open to the pain of loss, disappointment and even betrayal.

In the Anguttara Nikaya text, Buddha vividly sketches the un-satisfactory (dukkha) quality of life.

"Did you ever see in the world a man or a woman, eighty, ninety, or a hundred years old, frail, crooked as a gable-roof, bent down, supported on a staff, with tottering steps, infirm, youth long since fled, with broken teeth, grey and scanty hair, or bald-headed, wrinkled, with blotched limbs? And did the thought never come to you, that you also are subject to decay, that you cannot escape it?

Did you never see in the world a man or a woman, who being sick, afflicted and grievously ill, and wallowing in one's own filth, was lifted up by some people and put to bed by others? And did the thought never come to you, that you also are subject to disease, that you cannot escape it?

Did you never see in the world the corpse of a man or a woman, one or two or three days after death, swollen up, blue-black in color, and full of corruption? And did the thought never come to you, that you also are subject to death, that you cannot escape it?"(III.35)

This morose perspective is not merely the product of a melancholy disposition, for the Buddha has a sophisticated psychological and biological rationale for the pain which accompanies all human existence. The avenues by which these painful experiences travel are the five aggregates that we have already encountered; body, feeling, perception, disposition, and consciousness.

These five aggregates are the physiological and psychological faculties through which we both passively receive the world and actively partake in that world – the "person" or "self" is more identifiable with the aggregates or "bundles of experience" than with a traditional "ghost in the machine" type of soul. These aggregates of experience are the "organs" of pleasure and pain, and it is in relation to pleasure and pain that human craving can begin to arise. The Buddha summarizes the First Noble Truth in the Digha-Nikaya text.

"Birth is suffering; Decay is suffering; Death is suffering; Sorrow, Lamentation, Pain, Grief and Despair are suffering; not to get what one desires is suffering; in short: the Five Aggregates of Existence are Suffering."(22)

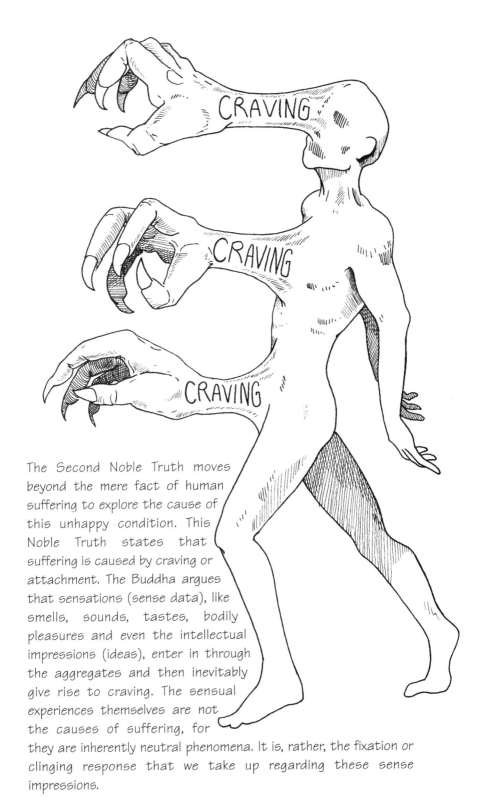

CRAVING

CRAVING

CRAVING

The Second Noble Truth moves beyond the mere fact of human suffering to explore the cause of this unhappy condition. This Noble Truth states that suffering is caused by craving or attachment. The Buddha argues that sensations (sense data), like smells, sounds, tastes, bodily pleasures and even the intellectual impressions (ideas), enter in through the aggregates and then inevitably give rise to craving. The sensual experiences themselves are not the causes of suffering, for they are inherently neutral phenomena. It is, rather, the fixation or clinging response that we take up regarding these sense impressions.

For example, it is not the sensual experiences which money affords us - fine food, fancy clothes, travel, new cars, etc - nor is it the material objects themselves that are inherently pernicious. It is the craving, wanting, desiring appetites, which become obsessed with repeating and sustaining those experiences, that actually cause the suffering, in this case, of greed. Suffering flows from clinging attachment which mistakes impermanent things and sensations for lasting and permanent realities. Attachment is a confusion, in the mind and the heart, that tries to capture or solidify that which is forever in flux.

In the Majjhima-Nikaya, Buddha develops the Second Noble Truth.

"If namely, when perceiving a visible form, a sound, odor, taste, bodily contact or idea in the mind, the object is pleasant, one is attracted, and if unpleasant, one is repelled. Thus, whatever kind of feeling one experiences - pleasant, unpleasant or indifferent - one approves of and cherishes the feeling and clings to it; and while doing so, lust springs up; but lust for feelings means clinging to existence; and on clinging to existence depends the process of becoming; on the process of becoming depends future birth; and dependent on birth are decay and death, sorrow, lamentation, pain, grief and despair. Thus arises this whole mass of suffering."(38)

The sensations that are always flowing in upon us become problematic only when we seek to hold on to the pleasant experiences – when we try to capture the ephemeral. Conversely, when we feel indignant and personally injured or offended by the unpleasant sensations, we have mistakenly reified our self into an object (soul) when we are really nothing but a process of changing aggregates. That is to say, we have made the mistake which Buddha believes the traditional Hindus have made; namely, we have forgotten that we too (our selves) are impermanent transitory realities. As an impermanent transitory reality, I can only be injured or indignant if I cling to myself, if I think of myself as a substance enduring through time. Craving, for the Buddha, is both an emotional passion and an intellectual misconception about reality. The suffering is caused when we falsely attribute "absolute" reality where there is only "relative" reality.

The Third Noble Truth states that the cure for suffering is non-attachment, or the cessation of craving. Freedom is not the renunciation of all emotions and feelings, it is the ability to rise above the incoming sensations. One still feels pain and pleasure, but one no longer clings to these fluctuating experiences. In the Dhammapada text, Buddha explains:

"The enlightened ones, at all times, surrender in truth all attachments. The holy spend not idle words on things of desire. When pleasure or pain comes to them, the wise feel above pleasure and pain"(83)

When the sensual perceptions and the mental ideas flow through the five aggregates that we conventionally call "Buddha," they continue flowing in their natural course without a clinging ego chasing after them. This detachment leaves no fertile soil for craving to take root. In the Samyutta-Nikaya text, Buddha explains that detachment stems from the philosophical realization of impermanence.

"Be it in the past, present or future: whosoever of the monks or priests regards the delightful and pleasurable things of this world as impermanent, miserable and without an Ego (anatman), as a disease and sorrow, it is he who overcomes the craving."(12;66)

"He who knows that this body is the foam of a wave, the shadow of a mirage, he breaks the sharp arrows of Mara (the personification of temptation), concealed in the flowers of sensuous passions and, unseen by Yama (the personification of painful death) he goes on and follows his path."(Dhammapada,46)

So, how does one put all this into practice? How, according to the Buddha, should we live our daily lives? What exactly is this "path" of the enlightened ones?

Noble Eightfold Path

This leads to the Fourth Noble Truth — which is really more like eight more truths masquerading as one. The cure for suffering, characterized in Truth Three as non-attachment, has eight steps or stages of practical realization — referred to as the Noble Eightfold Path. The Eightfold Path is a set of prescriptive attitudes and activities that will lead to the extinction of suffering, it is the path of freedom.

In the Samyutta Nikaya text, the Buddha
sets forth the facets of the holy path.

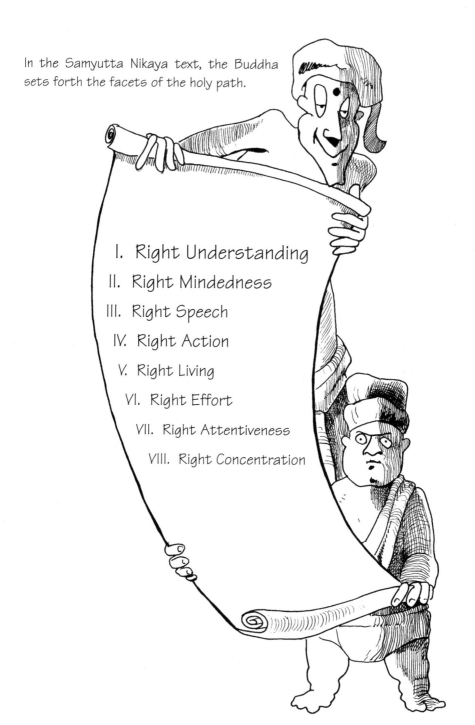

I. Right Understanding

II. Right Mindedness

III. Right Speech

IV. Right Action

V. Right Living

VI. Right Effort

VII. Right Attentiveness

VIII. Right Concentration

These eight maxims steer the searcher between the two pitfalls of extreme
indulgence on the one hand and extreme asceticism on the other. The eight
injunctions form the ethical details of that more general life-principle, the
Middle Way. It is worth exploring a few of the eight modes in greater depth.

Right Understanding: Similar to Socrates's famous position that the good life is the "examined" life, the Buddha believes that intellectual and emotional confusion must be grappled with on a daily basis. Right Understanding occurs when one pierces through the veil of naive consciousness (thinking of ourselves as Ego) to arrive at the true nature of things. The Buddha, and Socrates after him, understood that clarity of thought was most difficult regarding issues where the passions had a strong interest. One has to be especially vigilant for the temptations that can arise from the aggregate sensations.

Thus, in the Majjhima Nikaya text (9) and elsewhere, one finds fairly predictable lists of merit and demerit. Part of Right Understanding is sorting out demerits (destruction of living beings, stealing, lying, frivolous talk, etc.) from merits (abstaining from killing, abstaining from stealing, abstaining from lying, etc.).

What is more interesting than these piety lists, however, is that original Buddhism treats intellectual rigor as a virtue and ignorance as a sin. Some later sects of Buddhism have shared similar hostilities with Western Religions towards the intellect, claiming that ignorant faith is more important than logical thought. Right Understanding is the thoughtful discernment that helps a person see past the quick-fix gratifications to long-range karmic implications. Critical thinking, for the Buddha, is part of the moral path to freedom, for it allows one to recognize internal confusion.

"An enemy can hurt an enemy, and a man who hates can harm another man; but a man's own mind, if wrongly directed, can do him far greater harm." (Dhammapada,42)

Right Living: Many Western interpretations of Buddhism characterize the devotee as severely ascetic – refusing all pleasures and comforts – ultimately becoming a kind of unfeeling self-negating zombie. While some followers feel the need for such draconian measures, the Buddha himself never claimed that the path to enlightenment was self-torture.

NO THANKS, I'm STUFFED! THAT GRAIN OF RICE REALLY FILLED ME UP.

This makes perfect sense when we understand that pleasure and pain per se are inherently neutral, and immoral living arises only from the ego-attachments that tend to follow them. Therefore, one can enjoy – with moderation – all the earthly pleasures that any human has available. Poverty is not a necessary requirement for enlightenment, it is but another harmful extreme like opulence.

In the Anguttara-Nikaya text (2:70), Buddha explains that Right Living can contain prosperity if it is gained honestly without fraud or deception. Legitimately acquired wealth can be a source of happiness as long as greed (craving and ego-consciousness) does not throw one back into the quagmire of suffering. Economic prosperity can give one the happiness that accompanies freedom from debt. But that prosperity can not have injured another, for then it will not be able to give one freedom from blame.

Right Attentiveness : The early training that Gautama received in yoga meditation practice continued to play an important role in his mature philosophy. The Buddha, after all, had used these meditation practices that fateful day beneath the Bodhi Tree. Meditation is a deep form of psychological and physiological retraining, which allows one to perceive and reflect upon the facets of reality that are frequently masked and confused in the normal conscious state.

Intense concentration and profound tranquility blend together for the master yogi, and in this state she is reminded (through "experience" rather than discursive description) what freedom from worldly suffering is actually like.

Meditation is a method of inquiry that divides into four subjects of contemplation — these are the four fundamentals of attentiveness set forth in the Digha-Nikaya (22)

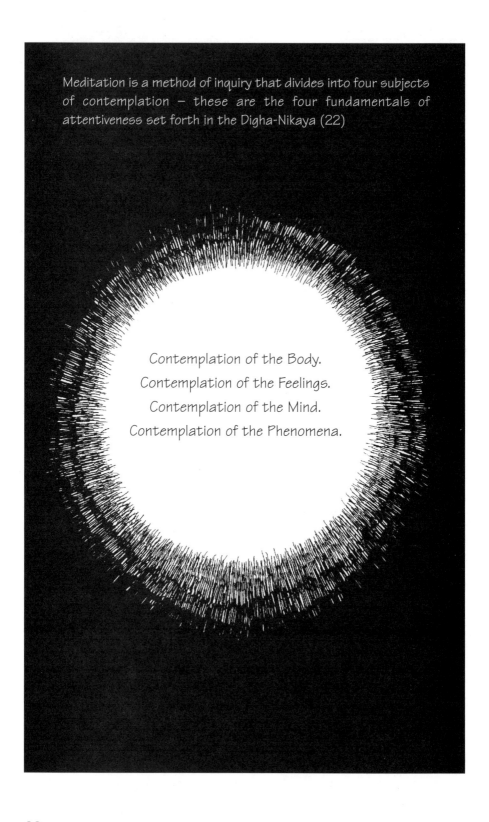

Contemplation of the Body.

Contemplation of the Feelings.

Contemplation of the Mind.

Contemplation of the Phenomena.

I. Contemplation of the Body: The Buddha recommends that the disciple find a quiet solitary place to sit, and with legs crossed and body erect, begin to focus upon the breathing process. After calming the bodily functions in this way, one is to focus attention towards the nature of body itself.

"Thus he dwells in contemplation of the body, either with regard to his own person, or to other persons, or to both. He beholds, how the body arises; beholds how it passes away; beholds the arising and passing away of the body.

A body is there—this clear consciousness is present in him, because of his knowledge and mindfulness, and he lives independent, unattached to anything in the world. Thus does the disciple dwell in contemplation of the body."

The disciple will contemplate the fact that the body is like a "sack with openings at both ends" filled with "hairs, nails, teeth, skin, flesh, bones, kidney, heart, lungs, bowels, stomach, excrement, bile, phlegm, pus, blood, sweat, tears, spittle, nasal mucus, oil of the joints, and urine." This meditation does seem to humble one if they are feeling particularly proud about their body.

With similar penetrating honesty the disciple continues with the fundamentals of attentiveness. II. Contemplation of the Feelings, III. Contemplation of the Mind, and IV. Contemplation of the Phenomena. And the Buddha summarizes the concept of Right Attentiveness in the Majjhima-Nikaya text (125).

"Just as the elephant hunter drives a huge stake into the ground and chains the wild elephant to it by the neck, in order to drive out from him his wonted forest ways and wishes, his forest unruliness, obstinacy and violence, and to accustom him to the environment of the village, and to teach him such good behavior as is required amongst men: - in like manner also has the noble disciple to fix his mind firmly to these four fundamentals of attentiveness, so that he may drive out of himself his wonted worldly ways and wishes, his wonted worldly unruliness, obstinacy and violence, and win to the True and realize Nirvana."

We have now examined, with some detail, three out of the eight steps of the Fourth Noble Truth. An important general point should now be raised regarding the overall character of Buddhist ethics.

The implementation of the Eightfold Path should not be carried out in a dogmatic legalistic fashion. The pathway is not an inflexible moral law dispensed from some otherworldly Judge, nor is it an unbending absolute duty dispensed from pure reason. As in the other areas of the Buddha's philosophy, here too the follower must attempt to avoid the lure of permanent absolutes.

Just as one is to refrain from viewing herself as eternal, so too one is to refrain from thinking of ethical codes as eternal. This does not lead the Buddha into the swamps of ethical relativism (yet another "extreme"). In other words, once the Buddha claims that ethical decisions are dependent upon the "context" within which they arise, he is not thereby thrown into an "anything-goes" morality. This is because the rightness or wrongness of any activity will be measured in terms of whether it respectively contributes to freedom (nirvana) or slavery (the wheel of becoming). And the same activity committed in two different contexts or by two different people can have two different implications for freedom. In this way, the Buddha's ethical philosophy has a liquid quality, an adaptability to situations. Ethics is the gateway to freedom, but if taken too dogmatically it can itself become a roadblock.

A classic example to illustrate the importance of context in moral activity is the following scenario. Imagine that you are living in Nazi occupied Europe and you are harboring a Jewish family in your basement.

Several SS officers making routine inquiries come to your door asking if you have seen any Jews in the vicinity.

Now, if the moral rule "Thou shalt not lie" is lived as an absolute — that is, as an inflexible law — one might be compelled to reveal the hidden family. But of course the deeper ethic should lead us to lie through our teeth.

JEWS EH? GOSH... NEVER HEARD OF 'EM. SORRY.

Compassion, not a legalistic duty, leads one to the right activity. This illustrates how a slavish dedication to doctrinaire morality has the potential to thwart true morality. And it is for these reasons that Buddha wants a Middle Way of context morality rather than the extremes of absolutism and relativism..

"Be moral and virtuous without being made of morals or virtues" (Majjhima-Nikaya 2.27) Compassion flows from the realization of human suffering and the impermanence of all things. Even our "enemies", for example, begin to arouse our compassion when we realize that they too are trapped by suffering. With this notion Buddha sought to rescue morality from the empty formalities of the Brahmins. Rules and rituals are blind without a cultivated heart of compassion.

Next we must examine the goal of the moral life, nirvana. Nirvana is one of those commonly invoked and commonly misunderstood concepts. The Buddha speaks of nirvana in two different senses; nirvana with the substrate (saupadisesa), and nirvana without the substrate (anupadisesa). We must sort out these two different forms of freedom.

Literally, nirvana means "going out" or "extinguishing" a flame, and we frequently find the Buddha playing with this image in his sermons. But what exactly is "going out" and what is this talk of a "substrate"?

In the Itivuttaka text, Buddha explains the concept of freedom with the substrate left. He describes the disciple who has effectively detached from his craving impulses, and he states that this individual has actually achieved freedom in this lifetime.

"He retains his five senses, through which, as they are not yet destroyed, he experiences pleasant and unpleasant sensations and feels pleasure and pain. This cessation of craving, hate, and confusion is called the nirvana with the substrate left."

Nirvana with substrate is living and experiencing through the five senses like everyone else, but no craving or confusion stems from those sense perceptions. "Substrate" refers to the underlying five aggregates that constitute each living person. Some interpreters have been confused about this form of nirvana, claiming that the Buddha is referring to the tranquil state of meditative trance that the trained yogi obtains. But on close examination, one finds this form of freedom characterized as an active life, one engaged in daily affairs.

The Buddha himself is an example of nirvana with the substrate left, because during his life he still functioned like any organism (via the five aggregates) yet he remained above the manipulations that frequently accompany these experiences.

"For he whose mind is well trained in the ways that lead to light, who surrenders the bondage of attachments and finds joy in his freedom from bondage, who free from the darkness of passions shines pure in radiance of light, even in this mortal life he enjoys the immortal nirvana." (Dhammapada,89)

In the Anguttara-Nikaya (III.53) Buddha again describes the individual, who has realized the ephemeral character of reality and recognized the traps of desire, as achieving freedom in this life time. "Thus is nirvana immediate, visible in this life, inviting, attractive and comprehensible to the wise."

ATTACHMENT

The usual course of events is that an impression, say "self satisfaction", enters into the individual and then ego-consciousness quickly leaps in to coddle and indulge the impression, thereby transforming it into "pride." One who lives nirvana is able to receive the impressions (the "substrate" of experience) but stop the second step — the entrance of the ego-consciousness. This violation of the usual course of events is possible because the person finally understands the causal mechanisms at work on and through her — she understands her own psychology. And through incredible discipline, she has practiced a lifetime of this detachment process. The Buddha actually describes this rare individual as the person "who goes upstream" rather than succumbing to the normal flow of attachment.

So, this form of nirvana is a kind of "transcendence" but it is not, contrary to some interpretations, transcendence to an otherworldly heaven. One psychologically rises above the muck and mire of mundane existence, but there is no ascension to a supernatural realm. This consideration leads us to the even more controversial form, nirvana without substrate.

In addition to the freedom attainable in this lifetime, the Buddha talks of an ultimate goal – often connected with the death of the enlightened person. This connection has led many, both later Buddhists and Western interpreters, to equate "nirvana without substrate" with an afterlife in a heavenly realm.

In the Dhammapada, Buddha describes this more complete form of freedom.

"The traveler has reached the end of the journey! In the freedom of the infinite he is free from all sorrows, the fetters that bound him are thrown away, and the burning fever of life is no more. He is calm like the earth that endures; he is steady like a column that is firm; he is pure like a lake that is clear; he is free from samsara, the ever returning life-in-death." (90,95)

One needs to be careful here about assuming a doctrine of heavenly immortality. Freedom with substrate means non attachment with sense impressions still passing through the body and consciousness, whereas freedom without substrate means that even these sense impressions have finally ceased. Thus nirvana in this case is not simply the "going out" or "extinguishing" of craving, it is the "going out" of all felt experiences. And it is here that the yogic trance does in fact give one the momentary cessation of all sense experience. That is to say, for brief periods the yogi can know what it is like to be dead — to be without substrate (the aggregates).

There is nothing, however, in this doctrine about surviving after death. Nonetheless, many of Buddha's disciples felt compelled at this precise juncture to ask about the afterlife – the issue seems to cry out for some speculation.

A student of the Buddha, Vacchagotta, asked the Master (Majjhima-Nikaya I: 483):

"Where does the enlightened person go after death?"

"It is impossible to say whether he is altogether annihilated or whether he is reborn again."

"But surely he continues on in some form or another?"

"Does a flame 'go somewhere' or 'continue' after it has burned all of its fuel?"

"No."

"Just as the fire is extinguished after all fuel is consumed, so too the enlightened one is extinguished after the aggregates (body, feeling, perception, disposition, and consciousness) are no more."

Ultimately, the Buddha is suggesting that it is absurd and meaningless to ask "Where does a flame go when it goes out?" And it is likewise absurd to engage in metaphysical speculation about events after death. Since we can not have a full experience of ourselves after death, we can not claim any real knowledge about this condition. The Buddha teaches that we must remain neutral on such questions and again walk the "middle way" between the dogma of afterlife belief and the dogma of annihilation. Indeed, so strong was Buddha's agnosticism about such metaphysical issues, that he even refused to say whether nirvana or freedom itself would last forever. Just as the sensual world and self are truly ephemeral, so too even freedom may be only transitory.

Chapter IV: The Evolution of Buddhism

THE BUDDHA DIED AROUND 480 BCE HAVING ALREADY WON MANY devotees with his compelling discourses. For approximately fifty years after his enlightenment he traveled the Ganges Valley teaching people that freedom from suffering was within their grasp. As he was dying, his closest friend Ananda expressed worries about how the community could continue the philosophy after the passing of the great Teacher. The Buddha responded by claiming that he had already taught them everything he knew – he had not held back any secrets. Therefore, he explained, the devotees would do fine without him. He said, "Ananda, be a lamp unto yourself, be a refuge unto yourself; seek not any outside help in this matter." His last words, like all his teachings, are infused by his overriding respect for human potential.

The historical Buddha affected several important philosophical revolutions during his lifetime. He challenged the ritualistic religions around him, arguing that morality and happiness are not the result of animal sacrifices and hollow ceremonial gestures. Ritual observance is only valid when it is an outward sign of an inner compassion.

He deplored the caste system and attempted to negate its pernicious bondage by arguing that the path to freedom is open to all who wish to pursue it. Nirvana recognizes no hierarchy but diligence.

The Buddha developed "the middle way" and thereby explained that neither asceticism (self-denial) nor hedonism (self-indulgence) is inherently righteous, because detachment is more achievable through moderation. Both self-indulgence and self-denial are too bound up with the "self" to be successful.

Finally, he tempered the metaphysical flights of those who squander their thoughts on the unknowable and those who invent spirits and egos where none exist. He refused to engage in scholarly debates about the afterlife and other such issues on the grounds that such issues are not open to experience, and they can distract one from the business of working out one's own enlightenment.

Shortly after the Buddha's death, the adherents began to fracture into diverse groups — each sect emphasizing a different nuance of the Teacher's message and life.

A series of councils met in the centuries after the Teacher's death to iron out doctrinal issues, the most famous of which seems to have been organized around 250 BCE by the converted emperor Asoka (circa 272-236).

According to legend, Asoka sent missionaries out of the Indian sub-continent, most notably South to Sri Lanka (Ceylon), and began the eventual spread of Buddhism throughout Asia. In Sri Lanka, the teachings of the Buddha were compiled into the Pali Canon (a corpus about ten times the length of the Bible), and it is these scriptures, divided into five groups or Nikayas, that seem to present us with the most accurate version of Gautama's teachings (together with the Chinese Agamas). Innumerably more texts, in various languages, have found their way into the Buddhist corpus over the centuries, and Buddhism has been radically transformed by every culture that embraces it. But the group that held fast to these earliest scriptures is usually referred to as Hinayana (the smaller path), and the most notable sub-sect (perhaps because it has endured in Southeast Asia) is known as the Theravada school (doctrine of the elders).

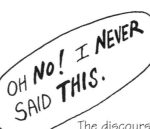

The discourses of the historical Buddha are collectively characterized as "dharma," but, as with most other great teachers, a set of subsequent texts began to arise after Gautama's death. These later texts are analyses of, and reflections on, the original dharma – they seem to be "secondary works" that found their way into the Buddhist Canon. These philosophical treatises are known as "abhidharma" (special dharma), and they quickly gave rise to deep divisions in the ranks of the faithful.

Besides Theravada, other early Hinayana schools include the Sarvastivada and the Sautrantika. Not only did these sects disagree about whether the dharma or abhidharma were primary or secondary sources of wisdom, they also began to divide strongly on metaphysical issues.

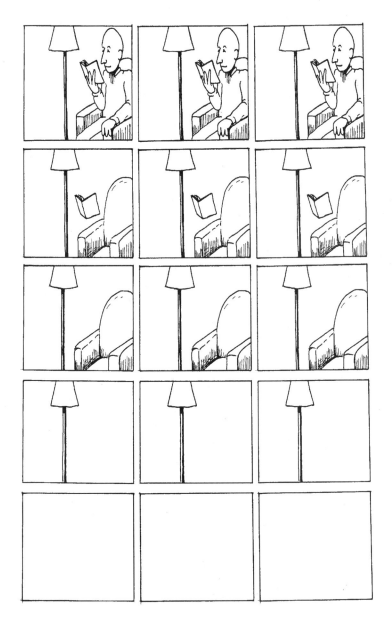

Trying to understand the Buddha's difficult doctrine of "no-self," the Sautrantikas argued that all moments follow each other with no underlying connection — each moment is completely unconnected to the previous moment and the future moment. The moments that you, the reader, spend reading this book seem to be tied together by the underlying identity of yourself — the reader seems to persist through the changes. But the Sautrantikas, following Buddha's rejection of the self, claim that there is no underlying identity from one moment to the next. Therefore, they conclude, there is no cause and effect relationship through time.

In a game of Billiards for example, one billiard ball seems to be caused to move by another earlier moving billiard ball, but in reality we have two completely isolated moments that happen to be joined together in time but share no causal communication with each other. But the denial of causality is dangerously close to a denial of karma, and as such this development in Buddhist philosophy may be seen as a suspicious departure from Gautama's original teachings.

The Sarvastivadins likewise struggled with these same issues and tried to explain how causality could still link moments together in a way that accounts for the regularity of nature which we readily observe. As we have seen, central to Buddhism is the idea of the impermanence of all things. Yet the world is not a chaos of unrelated moments haphazardly thrown together. Babies grow into adults, seasons follow one another predictably, and politicians become corrupt.

Sarvastivadins attempted to explain this phenomenon of continuity in the midst of impermanence by arguing that some "essence" or "substance" (svabhava) must persist through the alterations. In doing so, they fell back into the metaphysical trap of postulating semi-permanent entities that supposedly endure behind the curtain of impermanence. This metaphysical mistake is precisely the sort of error that led Hindus to postulate a spiritual ego (atman) behind their impermanent lives, and we have already seen that Gautama had no tolerance for this brand of mysticism.

Ultimately the Scholastic Buddhists of this ilk unwittingly sold out Gautama's emphasis on practical philosophy. Strains of Theravada Buddhism, however, have managed to avoid the pitfalls of bad metaphysics while remaining true to the practical wisdom of the early discourses. Perhaps the most definitive aspect of this ancient school is its focus upon the "teachings" of the Buddha, rather than the Buddha himself. The Theravada school has been less willing to take that tempting path which first turns Buddhism into hero-worship and ultimately deifies Gautama himself.

Contrasted with Hinayana Buddhism is the much more popular and heterogeneous school named Mahayana (the larger path). Most recent and contemporary Buddhist schools – Tantric Buddhism, Tibetan Lamaism, Chinese and Japanese "Pure Land" Buddhism, Zen and others – are descendants of the Mahayana movement.

Even in some of the earliest texts, the historical Buddha began to be characterized as "more than" a human being. Mystical embellishments, some quite recognizable to Westerners (e.g., virgin birth, devilish temptations, miraculous cures, and so on) became attached to Gautama's life. The Mahayana school, like most religions, had two dimensions – a popular ideology for the majority of devotees, and a more sophisticated set of doctrines and issues for the scholars. Both dimensions seem to have developed by focusing upon the metaphysical status of the Buddha himself.

Both during his own lifetime and after his death, questions regarding the uniqueness of the Buddha became important. How could such a great teacher be a mere human being? Will the Enlightened One pass from this mortal coil to a transcendental heaven after death? Is the Buddha a god in disguise?

Nagarjuna, who began the Madhyamika sect in the second century CE, was probably the most influential philosopher of the Mahayana school. He developed his philosophy by focusing on those questions that Gautama had refused to answer. When asked whether the enlightened person exists or not after death, the Buddha enigmatically responded by denying the four possible options — the enlightened one does exist, the enlightened one does not exist, the enlightened one both does and does not exist, and the enlightened one neither does nor does not exist.

From the fact that the Buddha rejected all these responses, Nagarjuna argued that language (and any method by which we try to represent reality) is unable to grasp the inexpressible infinite truth behind our limited experience. The Buddha, according to Nagarjuna, was purposely responding paradoxically in order to convey this deeper reality – the unspeakable Absolute. Like the Western theologians who argue that God's infinite nature is inexpressible and dimly understood by our finite natures, Nagarjuna argues that ultimate reality is ineffable or unsayable. Instead of calling this fundamental reality "God" and attributing personality traits to it, Nagarjuna refers to it as "emptiness" or "void" (sunya) to indicate its inexpressible character.

This concept of the ultimate "emptiness" of all things became an important notion in subsequent Mahayana philosophy, playing a particularly significant role in Tibetan Buddhism. Even in its earliest form however, the doctrine of "emptiness" becomes a metaphysical doctrine that exceeds the teachings of Gautama.

PHENOMENAL REALM

TRANSCENDENT ABSOLUTE

Some Mahayana philosophers argued that there were essentially "two worlds" — one, the day to day physical world of our experience and two, the transcendental unspeakable Absolute (or emptiness). The bridge between these worlds, they argued, was the Buddha himself — an incarnation of the transcendental Absolute which we finite humans could relate to in some fashion.

Of course, this is very similar to the Christian concept of an Earthly and a Heavenly realm with Jesus as a mediating go-between. In Christian theology, however, God reaches down to the human realm, but in this strain of Buddhism, a human reaches up to a non-personal transcendent Absolute.

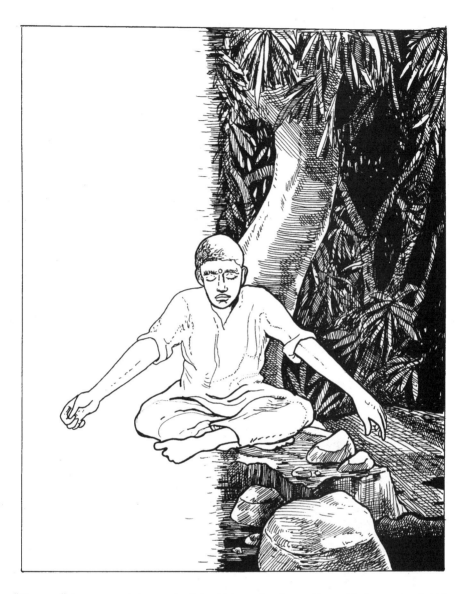

"Nirvana" becomes interpreted in this school as the attainment of this transcendent existence. The Yogacarins (a Mahayana sect flourishing around the 6th century BCE), for example, followed Nagarjuna's lead by rejecting this world of impermanence and embracing an Ideal Reality. The Yogacara school takes its name from its belief that yoga meditation can push the devotee beyond the natural world to this Ideal Absolute. In this sense, the Yogacarins went beyond the more skeptical and hesitant attitude of Nagarjuna, to proclaim with positive confidence their belief in a permanent Ideal Reality which they could actually meditate their way into. Once again, however, we seem to have more needless metaphysics here than Gautama would have appreciated.

Some Mahayana sects continued this deification of Gautama, but, as they did so, other characters began to populate their pantheon. That is to say, for some Mahayana Buddhists, particularly in popular Buddhism, there is not just one avatar, there are many. The historical Buddha repeatedly claimed that his elevated state of enlightenment was available to others, and that he was not utterly unique from other awakened ones (arhats or tathagatas). This empha-sis forces the devotee to avoid idolatry of the medium, and focus instead upon the message. Maha-yana Buddhism trans-forms this notion into the belief in "Bodhisattvas" (fledgling buddhas as it were). The idea of the Bodhisattva is an interesting develop-ment in the history of Buddhist philosophy because it reorients the devotee away from the individualistic goal of self-awakening towards the more socially responsible activity of helping oth-ers to gain new ground in the struggle. A Bodhisattva is a per-son who has liberated herself to the extent that she could pass into nirvana, but

chooses to stay in the world of suffering (samsara) in order to teach and aid others in the quest for freedom. Early descriptions of Bodhisattvas (e.g., the Prajnaparamita text) characterized them as human beings that had risen to a new level through their selfless compassionate devotion to others. This seems like a healthy amendment to the radical individualism of the early Buddhist ideal – the lone searcher striving for and winning nirvana for himself only.

An unfortunate byproduct of these amendments to early Buddhism is that these new spiritual teachers also went the way of Gautama's image – quickly degenerating into mythic idols for reverential worship. Buddhism developed a pantheon of divinities – deities to be intoned in times of trouble, to be sacrificed to, to be prostrated before, and to be bribed. Bodhisattvas, Buddhas and various other Saints increasingly became supernatural beings and as such increasingly distracted the average person from the business of freedom. In short, certain forms of Buddhism evolve into the very mistakes that Gautama fought against in Hinduism.

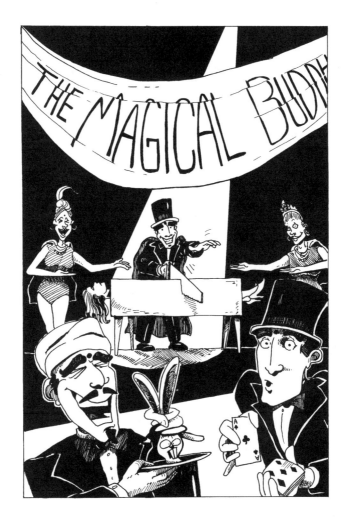

One of the forms most divergent from Gautama's teachings is probably the "Tantric" or magical sect of Buddhism. This form developed around the 6th or 7th century CE and it spread most notably to Tibet where it had a major influence. Tantric Buddhism further accentuates the trend, which began in the Mahayana schools, of separating average ordinary devotees from a rising class of supposed "gnostics" (an elite of people who are "in the know" regarding spiritual matters). The Tantric sect widens the gap between teacher and student until it becomes like a parent-child relationship of guru to pupil. Once the Tantric school divides people into camps of initiated and uninitiated, it quickly makes spiritual success dependent on one's subservience to a guru. This hierarchy is a distinct break from Gautama's message of equal-access freedom. Much of the historical Buddha's disgust with the caste system stems from his view that each human independently has the ability and the responsibility to perfect themselves.

Another aspect of Tantric thought that seems to run counter to early Buddhism is its strong emphasis upon magic. "Mantra" is Sanskrit for "spell" and Tantric Buddhism encouraged the practice of casting spells to protect oneself and generally influence the cosmos in one's favor. Chanting a phrase over and over has become a fairly significant aspect of some Buddhist schools, but it has little to do with original Buddhism. In addition to the practice of casting spells and dabbling in the occasional hex, the Tantric school engages in excruciatingly elaborate rituals. Complicated prayers and the sprinkling of holy water, for example, are aspects of some Tantric initiation rites.

There are two important reasons why this later development is not in step with, and may be quite inconsistent with, the historical Buddha's teachings. First, it seems rather unlikely that Gautama would agree to populate the cosmos with unseen ghosts and deities when he would not even agree to acknowledge his own soul. He showed himself to be hostile towards our strong tendency to postulate hidden agencies (most importantly, atman) where none could be confirmed. And more importantly, the existence or nonexistence of occult spirits has exactly no bearing whatever on the task of enlightenment. As the Buddha suggests, regarding a similarly insignificant metaphysical issue, there is no consequence to these matters because "there is still rebirth, there is old age, there is death, and grief, lamentation, suffering, sorrow and despair, the destruction of which even in this life I announce." (Majjhima Nikaya 63)

The second reason why the magical elements of later Buddhism seem contrary to Gautama's teachings is that they run counter to the laws of causality. According to early Buddhism, no amount of prayers, spells or ritual practices can reverse or mitigate the inexorable law of karma. Influencing the future is not done with prayerful entreaties or superstitious ceremonies, it is accomplished via the causal law by moral action. The practice of magical ceremonies designed to manipulate events presupposes the decidedly non Buddhist attitude that we are pawns in a fortuitous cosmic game. Through mystical rites one vainly hopes to negotiate with the causal law. But according to Gautama, there is only one way of perfecting oneself and eventually escaping the wheel of becoming, and it is accomplished through the annihilation of craving via the Eightfold Path.

Another important development in the history of Buddhism is the sect devoted to the supernatural Buddha named Amitabha. Amitabha, the Buddha of Infinite Light, is a divine being who lives in a heavenly paradise. This school's major text source is the Sukhavati Sutra, which describes this blissful promised land for devotees. Though originating in Northern India, the sect made great strides in China after the 7th century CE and Japan after the 10th century CE. In Japan, the school evolved into the "True Sect of the Pure Land" and continues to dominate Japanese Buddhism.

The sect's tremendous popularity is undoubtedly related to its simple and undemanding doctrine. Believe in Amitabha, and go to heaven; disbelieve, and you won't. No tortuous theology here, no rigorous yoga, no struggle for moral perfection.

Anyone, according to the Pure Land sect, who has faith (regardless of their moral worth or their social status) can be a Buddhist in good standing. Of course the "egalitarian" character of this sect is in tune with the historical Buddha's teachings, but just about everything else in the Pure Land school is rather discordant. "Faith" is not only uninteresting in early Buddhism, it is unintelligible. Unless one means by "faith", a belief in the efficacy of the Eightfold Path (and the Pure Land sect means significantly more by it), then it is hard to envision its meaning for Gautama. After all, there are no gods to have faith in, no rituals to blindly trust, no objects to venerate, no dogma to which to commit. For the historical Buddha, there is only Right Action and Right Understanding.

One last school worth touching upon is perhaps the most widely recognized in the United States, namely Zen Buddhism. "Zen" (Chinese "ch'an") means "meditation", and this Mahayana school took its lead from the Buddha's practice of contemplation. Zen seems to have begun in the 7th century CE in China and spread to Japan in the 13th century.

While it was in China, the movement certainly incorporated significant aspects of Taoism, one of the indigenous philosophies that emphasized harmony with nature. Zen adopts the Taoist idea that the "way" (tao) of effortless harmony is a meditative attitude which can transform daily activities (like drinking tea) into spiritual exercises.

There is also an emphasis, particularly in the Rinzai sub sect of Zen, upon the contemplation of irrational puzzles called "koans." One of the favorite koans, well known to many Westerners, is the question: "What is the sound of one hand clapping?" These riddles have an interesting connection with the earlier Mahayana philosophies of the Yogacarins. Both schools emphasized the act of meditation (quiet reflection or struggle with paradoxes) as a means of breaking down the ordinary concepts by which we organize our experience and letting our minds intuit the Ideal Reality. When the devotee escapes from thinking in terms of subjects and objects — dividing the world into artificial categories — she may achieve "satori" (sudden illumination) and this is a major step towards full enlightenment.

132

Most Zen schools are similar to early Buddhism in their rejection of tradition and scripture. The idea of Zen practice is to clear away all of the distractions of dogma and focus inwardly upon personal insight. Some schools, however, foster a strong dependence on a guru (Roshi) for spiritual progress, and this has the potential to degenerate into another Buddhist hierarchy. There are also Zen schools that continue to violate Gautama's stricture against excessive metaphysics by postulating an ultimate Ideal Consciousness as the fundamental reality.

Clearly Buddhism has undergone incredible changes since the time of Gautama. For two and half millennia Buddhism has been an evolving nest of ideas and practices.

By the 13th century CE, however, Buddhism ceased to play an important role in India, having been both driven out by Muslim invaders and assimilated back into Hinduism.

Though it continues to fall under persecution in nations like China, Vietnam, Tibet and North Korea, Buddhism remains a powerful if heterogeneous set of ideas.

One final issue in the philosophy and history of Buddhism needs to be examined. The role of women, both in early and later Buddhism, is an interesting story. Some have suggested that, when compared to other world religions, women fare pretty well in Buddhism. Indeed, there is much in the egalitarian tone of early Buddhist scriptures to suggest an enlightened view of women. Moreover, the early legends surrounding Gautama's life claim that he returned to his family after enlightenment and founded the first order of nuns – having been inspired by the wisdom of his Aunt Prajapati (step-mother).

In a rather bold break from tradition, the Buddha argued that women are equally capable with men of mastering their cravings and ultimately becoming enlightened ones. A monastic order of nuns was initiated and apparently thrived in India from the time of the Buddha until the 3rd or 4th century CE, after which it diminished drastically. The fate of women in Buddhism was foreshadowed in the earliest texts by confused and contradictory images, and the vacillating importance of asceticism.

We have already seen that Gautama's attitude towards asceticism is more sophisticated than the draconian measures of contemporaries like the Jains. Recall his argument that pleasures of the flesh were not inherently wicked. Instead, it was the turmoil of desire which could arise in the wake of pleasure that Gautama sought to destroy. Theoretically, one can affect this destruction even while experiencing pleasure. Nonetheless, the earliest monasteries, or groups of devotees, were to live according to a strict code of conduct called, The Rule. This Rule, which some attribute to Gautama himself, attempted to create an environment with little or no temptations to distract the devotee. Lust between the sexes was considered just another catalyst for craving, and every attempt was made in the monastic movements that followed Gautama's death to avoid this particularly strident bodily temptation.

The historical Buddha may have contributed to the ambivalence towards women by championing their right to, and capability for, "renunciation" on the one hand, but characterizing them in the Dhammapada (and other texts) as falling high on the list of things for monks to carefully avoid. Monks who were seeking to avoid the temptations of the sensual world demonized women into the symbols of all things earthly. Women seem to get this same rap wherever patriarchal structures mix with asceticism — in both Eastern and Western religions.

It is important to note, however, that it is only in the monastic Buddhist traditions (which quickly became male-dominant through preferential patronage) where this misogynist trend flourished. Unfortunately, the optimistic start which Gautama made by recognizing "female buddha-hood", was ultimately undone when Buddhism slowly melted back into the larger Hindu culture (Buddha was just recast as an incarnation of a Hindu god). The Hindu emphasis on social order, and individual conformity to that order, led the culture to look with *deep* suspicion and hostility upon a woman who was neither a wife nor a mother. Women following the asocial path of enlightenment were increasingly alone and without the needed support of the populace.

Some forms of the Tantric school (for all its other corruptions of early Buddhism) do seem to have taken a far healthier attitude towards the body, towards sexuality and towards women, than most other forms of Buddhism. Some Tantric mystic sects, probably drawing upon early Dravidian cultural influences, celebrate the female as a powerful cosmic principle. Male and female deities derive their mystical energies through sexuality, according to this theology, so why not us humans? Subsequently, sexuality actually becomes a vehicle for salvation, and gender relations take on a less bigoted tone.

Postscript

To actually examine the complex debates of early and later Buddhism is an eye-opening experience. For some time now, the West has been stereo-typing the East as a convenient "other" — a land of intuition and enigma. Philosophical traditions like Buddhism are seen as deeply irrational, inherently mysterious and ultimately inscrutable. Lamentably, this stereotype has been used by those Rationalist Westerners who hope to feel superior to the "backward" Eastern people. But more recently, the same stereotype is being employed by "New Age" Westerners to elevate irrationalism and mysticism — claiming Eastern intuitionism as the righteous path out of Western exploitation and alienation. One group shouts out Buddhism's difference from Western philosophy with derision in their voices, and the other group shouts out Buddhism's difference with adoration in their voices.

The irony of all this is that when one actually digs beneath the piles of self-improvement styled pop-spiritual dreck to find the original source material of both traditions, an astounding solidarity of common questions and methods emerges. Aristotle and the early Hinayana philosophers, for example, struggle with very similar questions of permanence and change in quite analogous ways. Or compare Gautama's and the Stoic Epictetus's moral philosophy, where a similar self mastery of the passions becomes the highest freedom in a world of servitude. In short, anybody who thinks that Buddhists are less rational than Westerners, should read their Nagarjuna. And anybody who thinks that Westerners are narrowly logistic, should read their Plato.

Some Further Reading

Primary Sources

Dialogues of the Buddha. C.A.F. Rhys Davids and T.W. Rhys Davids, trans. 3 vols. 5th ed. London: Luzac & Co. 1966.

The Book of Kindred Sayings. C.A.F. Rhys Davids and F.L. Woodward, trans. 5 vols. London: Pali Text Society 1917-1930.

Middle Length Sayings. I.B. Horner, trans. 3 vols. London: Pali Text Society 1954-1959.

Itivuttaka. E. Windish, ed. London: Pali Text Society 1948.

The Book of Gradual Sayings. F.L. Woodward and E.M. Hare, trans. 5 vols. London: Pali Text Society 1932-1936.

A Buddhist Bible. Dwight Goddard, ed. Boston: Beacon Press 1994 (orig. 1938, E.P. Dutton & Co).

Master of Wisdom: Writings of the Buddhist Master Nagarjuna. Christian Lindtner, ed. Dharma Publishing 1987.

Buddhist Wisdom Books. Edward Conze, trans. New York: Harper & Row 1958.

Secondary Sources

Buddhism: Its Essence and Development. Edward Conze. New York: Harper Torchbook 1959.

Women Under Primitive Buddhism. I.B. Horner. London: George Routledge 1930.

The Early Buddhist Theory of Man Perfected. I.B. Horner. London: Northgate & Williams 1936.

Women In Buddhism. Diana Y. Paul. University of California Press 1985.

Nagarjuna. The Philosophy of the Middle Way. David Kalupahana. Albany: State University of New York Press 1986.

Causality: The Central Philosophy of Buddhism. David Kalupahana. Hololulu: University Press of Hawaii 1975.

The Central Philosophy of Buddhism : A Study of the Madhyamika System. T.R.V. Murti. London: George Allen & Unwin 1955.

Indian Philosophy. S. Radhakrishnan. George Allen & Unwin 1962.

Index

Writers and Readers

> GREAT IDEAS AND GREAT THINKERS CAN BE THRILLING. THEY CAN ALSO BE INTIMIDATING AND COMPLICATED.

That's where **Writers and Readers For Beginners**™ books come in. **Writers and Readers** brought you the <u>very</u> <u>first</u> **For Beginners**™ book over twenty years ago. Since then, amidst a growing number of imitators, we've published some 70 titles (ranging from Architecture to Zen and from Einstein to Elvis) in the internationally acclaimed **For Beginners**™ series. Every book in the series serves one purpose: to UNintimidate and UNcomplicate the works of great thinkers. Knowledge is too important to be confined to the experts.

Plato For Beginners

by Rob Cavaliere
illustrated by Eric Lurio

Foucault For Beginners

by Lydia Alix Fillingham
illustrated by Moshe Susser

Clowns For Beginners

by Joe Lee

Saussure For Beginners

by W. Terrence Gordon
illustrated by Abbe Lub

Illustrations by Joe Lee, from **Clowns For Beginners**

SUBSTITUTE!

And knowledge, as you will discover in our "Documentary Comic Books," is fun! Each book is painstakingly researched, humorously written and illustrated in whatever style best suits the subject at hand.

> *MAKING*
> *COMPLEX SUBJECTS*
> *SIMPLE*
> *AND*
> *SERIOUS SUBJECTS*
> *FUN!!!*

That's **Writers and Readers**, where *For Beginners*™ books began! Remember, if it doesn't say...

... it's not an <u>original</u> *For Beginners* ™ book!

Chomsky For Beginners

by David Cogswell; illustrated by Paul Gordon

Race For Beginners

by S.E. Anderson Illustrated by The Cro-Maat Collective

McLuhan For Beginners

by W. Terrence Gordon; illustrated by Susan Willmarth

I-Ching For Beginners

by Brandon Toropov; illustrated by John Kane

The History of Eastern Europe For Beginners

by Beck, Mast and Tapper

HOW TO GET GREAT THINKERS TO COME TO YOUR HOME...

To order any current titles of Writers and Readers **For Beginners**™ books, please fill out the coupon below and enclose a check made out to **Writers and Readers Publishing, Inc.** To order by phone (with Master Card or Visa), or to receive a <u>free catalog</u> of all our **For Beginners**™ books, please call (212) 982-3158.

Price per book: $11.00

Individual Order Form
(clip out or copy complete page)

Book Title	Quantity	Amount
	Sub Total:	
N.Y. residents add 8 1/4% sales tax		
Shipping & Handling ($3.00 for the first book; $.60 for each additional book)		
	TOTAL	

Name _____

Address _____

City _____ **State** _____ **Zip Code** _____

Phone number ( ) _____

MC / VISA (circle one)   Account # _____ **Expires** _____

Send check or money order to: **Writers and Readers Publishing**, P.O. Box 461 Village Station, New York, NY 10014 (212) 982-3158, fx (212) 777-4924; In the U.K: **Airlift Book Company**, 8, The Arena, Mollison Ave., Enfield, EN3 7NJ, England 0181.804.0044. Or contact us for a <u>FREE CATALOG</u> of all our *For Beginners*™ titles.